Purple Ronnie's

Little Book for a

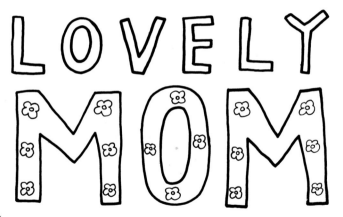

LOVELY MOM

by Purple Ronnie

Based on and adapted from the work entitled Purple Ronnie's Little Book for
a Lovely Mum first published in the United Kingdom in 2006 by Pan Macmillan
Publishers Ltd.

08 09 10 11 12 TEN 10 9 8 7 6 5 4 3 2

ISBN-13: 978-0-7407-7117-0
ISBN-10: 0-7407-7117-5

Library of Congress Control Number: 2007934067

"Purple Ronnie" created by Giles Andreae. The right of Giles Andreae and Janet
Cronin to be identified respectively as the author and illustrator of this work
has been asserted by them in accordance with the Copyright, Designs, and Patents
Act 1988. This edition of Purple Ronnie's Little Book for a Lovely Mom is
published by arrangement with Purple Enterprises Limited, a Coolabi company.

www.andrewsmcmeel.com

Interesting Fact

Moms are absolute experts at doing hundreds of things all at the same time

Rules of Being a Mom - N°1

Once in a while, it's good just to really spoil yourself

Some moms are more than just moms—they're best friends as well

☆ Special Tip
_____

Never trust a mom
whose kitchen is too tidy

Rules of Being a Mom - № 2

When you become a mom, you will not get a proper night's sleep for about 20 years

Pants

When you are a mom you are allowed to wear big pants even if your bottom is actually quite small

☆ Special Tip for Moms

Make sure your man is as
well trained as possible

Rules of Being a Mom - N°3

From now on, at least half of your life will be spent in the car

☆ Special Tip for Moms

Sometimes chocolate is very, very helpful indeed

There is nothing a mom loves more than a really good gossip with her friends

Rules of Being a Mom - Nº 4

Every year it gets more difficult to make your tummy look like it used to

Some moms find it hard to get dads away from watching the T.V.

☆ **Special Tip**

Try to make a bit of time
for yourself every day to do
what you want to do

Rules of Being a Mom - Nº 5

Your kitchen is a free restaurant and you are the cook, the waitress, and the cleaner

Sometimes moms get worried that being a mom makes their brains turn to jelly

☆ <u>Special Tip</u>

Never tell a mom that you love her squidgy bits - even if you're trying to be nice

Rules of Being a Mom - N° 6

Suddenly you see the point of shops you never used to understand

CHEAP AND CHEERFUL
SOFT + COMFY SHOES
hurry up!
Stretchy waists!
BIG COTTON PANTS
natter
drag
DESIGNER SHOES

Sometimes, not even the fanciest restaurants can beat mom's home cooking

Moms love nothing more
than looking at old
photos of their little
darlings

Rules of Being a Mom - N°7

Sometimes it's best just to let your man get on with it and try not to laugh

Special Tip

Sometimes moms need a little bit of extra help to get them through the day

☆ Special Tip

Give your mom a little
treat once in a while and
she will think you are
amazing

Rules of Being a Mom - N° 8

However much you try not to, sometimes you end up sounding exactly like your own mom

you are absolutely not going out in that dress!
Moooom!
sulk
DAUGHTER...
...MOM...
...WEIRD TIME LOOP....

wise words
there there
Barry doesn't like me any more
Kevin ate my pet spider!
wail
boo hoo

Sometimes moms have to have very long arms indeed

Some moms love nothing
better than a really good
session in the garden

champion ref
He poked me in the eye!
Well, she scribbled on my pants

Rules of Being a Mom · Nº 9

You must be even better at settling arguments than a wrestling referee

☆ <u>Warning</u>

When you become a mom,
your shopping list
completely changes

Sometimes even moms
need a little bit of
peace and quiet

Rules of Being a Mom - Nº 10

However much a mom gets done in a day, there is always something more to do

Remember ♡

Most moms are really angels in disguise